DRAMA

The Drama ~~ series~~ ... greatest pl~~a~~ ~~i~~n affordable p~~rice~~ ...ns fo... actors and theatregoers. Th~~e~~ ~~aim~~ ~~of the~~ ser~~ie~~s are accessible introductions, ~~abo~~ut ~~read the work~~ an overall theatrical perspective.

Given that readers may be encountering a particular play for the first time, the introduction seeks to fill in the theatrical/historical background and to outline the chief themes rather than concentrate on interpretational and textual analysis. Similarly the play-texts themselves are free of footnotes and other interpolations: instead there is an end-glossary of 'difficult' words and phrases.

The texts of the English-language plays in the series have been prepared taking full account of all existing scholarship. The foreign-language plays have been newly translated into a modern English that is both actable and accurate: many of the translators regularly have their work staged professionally.

Edited until his early death by Kenneth McLeish, the Drama Classics series continues with his aim of providing a first-class library of dramatic literature representing the best of world theatre.

Associate editors:
Professor Trevor R. Griffiths
Dr. Colin Counsell
School of Arts and Humanities
University of North London

DRAMA CLASSICS *the first hundred*

The Alchemist
All for Love
Andromache
Antigone
Bacchae
Bartholomew Fair
The Beaux Stratagem
The Beggar's Opera
Birds
Blood Wedding
Celestina
The Changeling
A Chaste Maid in Cheapside
The Cherry Orchard
Children of the Sun
El Cid
The Country Wife
The Dance of Death
The Devil is an Ass
Doctor Faustus
A Doll's House
Don Juan
The Duchess of Malfi
Edward II
Electra (Euripides)
Electra (Sophocles)
An Enemy of the People
Everyman
Faust
A Flea in her Ear
Frogs
Fuente Ovejuna
The Game of Love and Chance
Ghosts
The Government Inspector
Hecuba
Hedda Gabler

The Hypochondriac
The Importance of Being Earnest
An Ideal Husband
An Italian Straw Hat
Ivanov
The Jew of Malta
The Knight of the Burning Pestle
The Lady from the Sea
The Learned Ladies
Lady Windermere's Fan
Life is a Dream
London Assurance
The Lower Depths
The Lucky Chance
Lulu
Lysistrata
The Malcontent
The Man of Mode
The Marriage of Figaro
Mary Stuart
The Master Builder
Medea
The Misanthrope
The Miser
Miss Julie
A Month in the Country
Oedipus
The Oresteia
Peer Gynt
Phedra
The Playboy of the Western World
The Recruiting Officer
The Revenger's Tragedy

The Rivals
The Roaring Girl
La Ronde
Rosmersholm
The Rover
Scapino
The School for Scandal
The Seagull
The Servant of Two Masters
She Stoops to Conquer
The Shoemakers' Holiday
Six Characters in Search of an Author
The Spanish Tragedy
Spring Awakening
Summerfolk
Tartuffe
Three Sisters
'Tis Pity She's a Whore
Too Clever by Half
Ubu
Uncle Vanya
Volpone
The Way of the World
The White Devil
The Wild Duck
A Woman of No Importance
Women Beware Women
Women of Troy
Woyzeck
Yerma

The publishers welcome suggestions for further titles

DRAMA CLASSICS

ELECTRA

by

Sophocles

translated and introduced by
Marianne McDonald and J. Michael Walton

NICK HERN BOOKS

London

www.nickhernbooks.co.uk

A Drama Classic

Electra first published in Great Britain in this translation
as a paperback original in 2004 by Nick Hern Books Limited,
14 Larden Road, London W3 7ST

Typeset by Country Setting, Kingsdown, Kent CT14 8ES
Printed and bound in Great Britain by Bookmarque,
Croydon, Surrey

This translation arises out of the work of the Performance
Translation Centre in the Drama Department at the
University of Hull, HU6 7RX

A CIP catalogue record for this book is available
from the British Library

ISBN 1 85459 756 6

Introduction

Sophocles

Sophocles was the second of the great Athenian dramatists. He was said to have been born around 496 BC and to have died in 406 BC, soon after Euripides, his contemporary and rival. Born at Colonus, the setting for his final play, *Oedipus at Colonus,* Sophocles lived through the Athenian defeat of the Persians in two major battles, Marathon in 490 and Salamis in 480. Much involved in public affairs, in 443/2 he became a treasurer, or *Hellenotamias*, of the Delian League, a confederacy of independent city-states which Athens headed after the Persian wars.

He was elected a general to put down the revolt of Samos, one of the members of the League, in or around 441. The bodies of the dead were exposed, as enemies often were, and it was possibly here that Sophocles became interested in heroes and heroines who wanted to bury the dead (for example, Teucer in *Ajax*, and Antigone in the play that bears her name, both written about the time of the Samian War). Another theory claims that he was awarded this generalship on the strength of having written *Antigone*. In 413, during the Peloponnesian War against Sparta (431-404 BC), he was elected one of the *Probouloi*, special officials appointed to deal with the aftermath of the Sicilian defeat.

Late in his life, it is said that he was sued for incompetence in managing his affairs by one of his children. He won the day by reciting a chorus from *Oedipus at Colonus*, which he was writing at the time. At the Greater Dionysia of 406, shortly after the death of Euripides, he took part in the dramatic competition and dressed all his actors in mourning to honour Euripides. He himself died later that year, before the final Athenian defeat by the Spartans in 404, and was spared seeing his city's final humiliation. *Oedipus at Colonus* was performed posthumously in 401 BC.

After his death, Sophocles was revered as *Dexion*, a type of healing spirit associated with Asclepius, whose worship he had introduced to Athens after the plague at the beginning of the Peloponnesian War. He was also a priest of the healing god, Halon.

Tragedy and Comedy in Athens were presented in competition at two major religious festivals in honour of the god Dionysus. Sophocles' first dramatic victory, we are told, was in 468, in competition against Aeschylus. In all, Sophocles wrote about 120 plays, more than any of the other playwrights (Euripides writing about 90 and Aeschylus about 80). He often won first prize, sometimes second, but never third. He was the most successful and popular playwright of the three great tragedians: Aeschylus was said to have won about thirteen victories, Euripides, four, and Sophocles over twenty, possibly twenty-four. We are told Sophocles had a weak voice, and so did not act in his own plays, as Aeschylus had, but he did lead a chorus once.

Of the surviving seven plays, only *Philoctetes* and the *Oedipus at Colonus* can be dated with certainty, and the *Antigone* approximately, if we accept a connection with the Samian War. The following chronology is tentatively suggested:

Antigone	ca. 443-440 BC
Ajax	ca. 442 BC
Women of Trachis	ca. 430s BC
King Oedipus	ca. 420s BC

Electra	ca. 425-413 BC
Philoctetes	**409 BC**
Oedipus at Colonus	**401 BC** (performed posthumously)

There are fragments of many other plays, including a large part of the satyr play, the *Ichneutae* (*The Trackers*).

What Happens in the Play

Legend tells us that King Agamemnon fought a war at Troy to recover Helen, his brother's wife, who had been stolen by Paris, a prince of Troy. To secure favourable winds, he sacrificed his daughter, Iphigenia. While he was away at Troy, his queen, Clytemnestra, took a lover, Aegisthus, and plotted to kill Agamemnon on his return, which she did after luring him into a bath. Electra, Iphigenia's sister, rescued her brother, Orestes, and gave him to the family Tutor to bring to Strophius, who would raise him in Phocis out of harm's way. Orestes grew up with Pylades, the son of Strophius.

At the beginning of Sophocles' play, Orestes enters with Pylades and the Tutor. Orestes has consulted Apollo, who told him that he should take vengeance on Aegisthus and Clytemnestra by stealth. Orestes sends out the Tutor to reconnoitre. They will bring a false story of Orestes' death in a chariot race. Orestes will make offerings at Agamemnon's tomb, enlisting the help of his dead father. Orestes leaves with Pylades.

Electra appears, grieving for her father. Her lamentations are in lyric metres and would have been sung in the original. The Chorus show themselves to be Electra's allies in the desire to punish the ruling tyrants. However, the Chorus advise Electra she is mourning too much. She rejects them, on the grounds that such advice is ignoble. She as a noble woman will never give up her ideals, or cease to mourn her father and plan the destruction of the new rulers.

The Chorus warn her that wandering outside the house and making seditious remarks can only bring her harm. Chrysothemis enters and urges her sister to comply with the rulers. Electra answers her with contempt and calls her a coward. Chrysothemis reveals that Clytemnestra and Aegisthus are planning to send her away if Electra continues acting as she is. Electra says she would welcome this, because she is sick of Chrysothemis and others who advise her to curb her public complaints.

Chrysothemis is carrying offerings for Agamemnon, which Electra learns were sent by Clytemnestra. Clytemnestra has had a bad dream of Agamemnon's sceptre growing larger until its branches and leaves cover all of Mycenae. Electra hopes that the dream is favourable to her cause and advises Chrysothemis not to make the offerings, as they would be construed by their father as an insult since they were sent by his murderer.

Clytemnestra confronts Electra and gives as her excuse for the murder of Agamemnon the killing of their daughter Iphigenia. (In Aeschylus' *Agamemnon*, Clytemnestra added two more reasons: Cassandra, the mistress whom Agamemnon brought home; and her inevitable fulfilment of the family curse which afflicted the house of Atreus.)

Clytemnestra asks why her child had to be sacrificed rather than Menelaus', since it was his wife they were trying to regain. Electra answers by saying that Artemis commanded this sacrifice. Agamemnon killed her sacred stag and boasted about it. To gain favourable winds and win the war, he was compelled to kill his child.

Electra asks her mother why she killed her father, married a lover and had children by him, while neglecting the children she already had. Clytemnestra is furious and threatens her with what will happen as soon as Aegisthus returns home.

The Tutor enters and tells an elaborate story of a chariot race at the Pythian Games in which, he says, Orestes was killed. The account is breathtakingly graphic and convinces both Electra and Clytemnestra. Clytemnestra is in part relieved but laments that her safety is bought with pain: even when children treat a parent badly they are still loved. She takes the Tutor indoors.

Chrysothemis arrives with news that she believes Orestes has returned, because of fresh grave offerings she found on Agamemnon's tomb. Electra tells her she is a fool and informs her about the report she has just heard. She tries to enlist Chrysothemis's help in taking vengeance, telling her of the freedom and admiration they will gain, and how easily Chrysothemis will find a fine husband to marry. Chrysothemis refuses and Electra accuses her again of being a disloyal coward: 'A shameful life shames nobility'.

Orestes enters with Pylades. Electra asks to hold the urn he brings which he tells her contains her brother's ashes. An emotional lament follows. Orestes is so moved by her grief that he reveals himself, showing her a signet ring which belonged to their father.

Electra celebrates her brother's arrival with an enthusiasm as excessive as was her mourning. The Tutor appears from indoors to say that they are making too much noise and risk having their plot revealed.

Clytemnestra is alone indoors, so they all go inside the palace. Electra comes out again to watch for Aegisthus. Clytemnestra screams as she is stabbed, but Electra tells Orestes to strike again if he can. Aegisthus arrives, having heard of Orestes' death and asks to see the body.

The doors open to reveal Orestes and Pylades with a body
under a sheet. Aegisthus uncovers it only to discover
Clytemnestra. Orestes says that he will take Aegisthus inside
to kill him. Electra suggests that his body be thrown out of
the house. At the end of the play Orestes says, 'Every
criminal should be punished by death/And without delay.
Then we'd have less crime.'

The Chorus celebrates the victory at the end and the
freedom attained, albeit costly.

Electra

The story of Electra is the only surviving example we have of
the same plot written in different versions by all three of the
great Athenian tragedians, Aeschylus, Sophocles and
Euripides. There is a play called *Electra* by Euripides as well
as one by Sophocles. The date of both of these is uncertain,
and critics, including the present editors, disagree about
which came first. Both were probably performed between 428
and 413 BC, but perhaps much closer in time so that one of
them could have been seen by the first audiences as a direct
response to the other. Both were written with an awareness
of, and to some extent as a riposte to, Aeschylus' *Oresteia*,
produced in 458 BC, two years before the poet's death. The
Oresteia is a trilogy, three plays of which the middle one,
Libation-Bearers, covers almost exactly the same span of time as
do the Electra plays of Sophocles and Euripides. The
treatment of all three is highly individual.

Aeschylus offers a broader view of the saga, from the return
of Agamemnon after the fall of Troy and his murder by his
wife Clytemnestra and Aegisthus (*Agamemnon),* through the
revenge of Orestes and Electra (*Libation-Bearers*), and on into the
third play, *Eumenides,* in which Orestes is tried for matricide

at the Court of the Areopagus in Athens, and acquitted. So we can say, with confidence, that both later playwrights and their first audiences would have had some idea of the outlines of the plot as presented on stage before, but were interested from a dramatic and theatrical standpoint in the variations that could be worked on how the story was treated. Euripides also wrote several plays on other aspects of the story, two about Iphigenia and one called *Orestes* set after the revenge. Between 458 BC (the date of the *Oresteia*) and the two *Electras* great changes had taken place in Athens, both politically and socially. These are reflected in the context and priorities of tragedy as the playwrights placed more emphasis on character and began to experiment with the possibilities of the stage. Audiences, too, came to apprecaite new approaches.

This *Electra* is vintage Sophocles, concentrating on the plight of the central figure Electra, whose treatment by her mother and new husband is played out against, and almost in spite of, the audience's awareness that Orestes has returned and is putting into operation the plot to kill the oppressors. The complaints of brother and sister are valid ones and, if one believes that wrongdoing should be punished and the gods obeyed, Orestes and Electra are morally vindicated. The position that the play appears to endorse has seemed more dubious to later generations. Some scholars believe that Sophocles is being ironic throughout and that he is showing what evil creatures this brother and sister are to murder their mother. But this seems to be reading Sophocles as though he were Euripides. Euripides' *Electra* shows a sordid duo carrying out a brutal murder. In that play, even the oracle from Apollo is called evil.

Aeschylus had fully appreciated the terrible consequences of murdering one's mother. The Furies descended on Orestes to punish him: only a trial presided over by Athena was able to resolve the impasse. But there is a crucial difference between Aeschylus and Euripides: the former believed in the justice of Zeus, complicated though it may be. Euripides could make the gods more vindictive and irrational than man; justice at times seems irrelevant.

Sophocles is a master of dramatic tension, in every aspect of the build-up to the murders, even in the fictive story of Orestes' death during an exciting chariot race. Orestes is a paragon of honour in contrast to the Orestes in Euripides' play, who conceals himself until discovered, and who kills Aegisthus with a cowardly blow from behind after being invited to a sacred feast. Sophocles' Orestes is prudent, pious – he first visits his father's grave – but dedicated to avenging his father as Apollo has commanded him. Electra shows the emotionalism which women were thought to possess, but is portrayed as a noble character reduced to near-despair by the years of abuse she has suffered. Passionate and dedicated to her father, she is admirable in her loyalty, however shocking her urging Orestes to strike their mother yet again.

Sophocles is showing us exactly what it means to 'Help your friends and harm your enemies', an old maxim which can be traced to Homer. A fight in war is a fight to win. It does no harm to embrace a cause. Electra and Orestes are dedicated warriors and Sophocles wants them to be seen in that way. In this, his treatment is much more Homeric than that of either of the other playwrights.

One way that he does this is through the ordering of the murders. His is the only play that ends with Aegisthus's death *after* that of Clytemnestra, a decision which disarms the lack of debate over the morality of matricide. However, the issue is still with us today as to whether loyalty to a father can justify such revenge.

Good but not conclusive arguments can be made on either side. What is clear is that both Sophocles and Euripides wanted to write plays that were different from any previous version. Sophocles celebrates the heroism of man, whereas Euripides shows the sordidness of victory when it involves killing another human being. One accepts the gods; the other questions them if they condone murder being repaid by murder.

Euripides was an anti-war playwright who celebrated the victim rather than the victor. Both Clytemnestra and Aegisthus in his *Electra* show themselves superior to their slayers. Clytemnestra for Euripides was a caring mother and Aegisthus a welcoming host. Electra in that play seems more concerned about losing her inheritance than about losing her father. Sophocles' Electra is more concerned about her father and the way that he was dishonoured. His slayers deserve punishment. Sophocles wrote a cruel play as Homer had written cruel epics. As is said in the play, 'Sometimes being right is dangerous'.

The repetition of expressions of grief seems strange on the page, but Sophocles offers a musical structure, and it should never be forgotten that the lyric passages would all have had musical accompaniment. The most moving arias in the play are sung by Electra, culminating in her lament over the urn. Her sister, Chrysothemis, shows herself as a believable character, arguing for moderation and being more concerned about her own marriage and circumstances than about vengeance, although she admits that Electra has a just cause. The Chorus are similarly loyal to Electra and interject pleas for moderation from time to time that make a lot of sense but fall on deaf ears. The language is brilliantly metaphorical: Sophocles shows himself a master of poetry to equal Aeschylus.

This play is rightly considered one of the world's masterpieces, revived again and again. It is no accident that

Sophocles inspired Hugo von Hofmannsthal to write his play of the same name. Richard Strauss turned Hofmannsthal's play into one of the great modern operas in which Electra's passion culminates in a type of apotheosis when she dances herself to death in ecstasy over their victory.

Sophocles and his Philosophy

Sophocles was the playwright of heroism, which he celebrates with Homeric vigour. All the Greeks of his time were brought up on the battles in the Homeric epics, *The Iliad* and *The Odyssey*. Sophocles added dramatic characterisation to the Homeric heroes and showed their obsession with honour. As Ajax says, 'The noble person either lives with honour, or dies with it' (*Ajax*, 479-80), and we hear similar words from Electra.

Another play by Sophocles which shows heroic action is *Antigone* (ca. 443-440). Antigone is the first conscientious objector, and the first true heroine in Western literature. Some would call her a martyr. In any case, she gained glory from her choice to bury her brother against the law of the state as she defended 'the unwritten laws of the gods'. Freedom fighters ever since have been evoking her example.

Sophoclean heroes and heroines are not likeable people in the ordinary sense of the word. One can admire them, but would hardly want to live with them. This certainly holds for Electra and Orestes in this play. Sophocles believed in law and order, and a justice from the gods, which man must strive to understand, because his gods do not make the task easy. The single-minded heroes and heroines seem to go too far in everything they do, violating the maxim on the temple at Delphi: 'Nothing in Excess'. They can even bring down the innocent in defence of their principles, as did Antigone. But their greatness cannot be challenged. As Bernard Knox wrote, 'Sophocles creates a tragic universe in which man's heroic action, free and responsible, brings him sometimes through suffering to victory but more often to a fall which is both defeat and victory at once; the suffering and glory are fused in an indissoluble unity.' This might serve as a definition for all tragedy.

Sophocles celebrates the greatness of mankind. In spite of the most terrible tragedy that the gods send, these heroes have a spirit which is able to match it. In Sophocles, the power and glory belong to men and women willing to die for their honour. His plays are paeans to the human spirit.

Original Staging

Athenian plays were usually performed in the fifth-century theatre of Dionysus in Athens which was outdoors, and featured a circular playing area called the *orchêstra*. It may have had an altar in the centre. It was built into the side of the hill that culminated in the Acropolis on which the Parthenon stands.

This theatre seated about 15,000 to 18,000 people, from a population of about 300,000 in Attica, comprised of male citizens, women, children, slaves and foreign residents. It is not known for sure whether women attended the theatre, though they did in the following century.

The main Athenian dramatic festival was called the Greater Dionysia, in honour of the god of theatre, Dionysus. The Greater Dionysia was held in early spring, the 9th-13th days of the month *Elaphêboliôn* (March/April), when the seas were calm and Athenian allies and foreign traders and diplomats could safely make the sea journey. On the first day there was an elaborate show of tribute from the allies, war orphans

were paraded, and prominent citizens were given awards.
Going to the theatre was a social, civic and religious event.
The city was on show, and the mood of the city was on
show. One purpose of the festival was to impress foreigners.

Three or four days of the Greater Dionysia were devoted to
plays. The performances began at first light and lasted all
day. There are several plays whose action begins at dawn, or
even in the dark.

Three playwrights were selected by a state official (*archôn*) in
early autumn to put on three tragedies and one satyr play
that comically handled tragic themes. This process was
known as 'awarding a chorus' and ensured some state
support and finance. The rest of the production costs were
met by a kind of semi-compulsory patronage known as the
chorêgia, undertaken by private citizens. After the tragedians'
group of four, the audience could enjoy political comedies,
like those of Aristophanes, which were played, either one on
the same day as the tragedies, or several on a separate day
simply devoted to comic performance.

Soon after Aeschylus began to present plays, a prize was
given for the best tragic playwright and, later in the century,
one for the best writer of comedy. The audience, who paid to
attend, were closely involved with the performance and
reputed to have openly expressed their feelings and reactions.
The *chorêgos*, who paid for the costuming and training of the
chorus, was also given a prize if his playwright won. The jury
was selected, one from each of the ten tribes, but only five
votes from the ten were randomly selected to decide the
winner. This helped to avoid jury-tampering.

All the actors, including the chorus, were male and masked,
playing both male and female roles. The masks were quite
realistic but demanded a very physical kind of acting.

Characters could be recognised by the audience from emblematic costume or properties. At first all the actors were amateur, and the playwright acted too. Eventually acting became professional, and prizes were then awarded to the best actor at the festival. It may well have been Thespis as the first actor, who added prologue and speech to choral performance before Aeschylus was born. Aristotle writes that Aeschylus added a second actor and Sophocles a third: doubling of roles seems to have remained the norm.

The chorus in Aeschylus probably numbered twelve but this number rose to fifteen in Sophocles and Euripides, twenty-four for the comedies of Aristophanes. After their initial entrance the chorus usually stayed on stage until the end. The word *choros* means 'dance', *orchêstra* 'dancing-place', and their movements were accompanied by the *aulos*, a reed instrument (like an oboe), and sometimes drums. Spoken portions of the drama, mainly in iambic trimeter (a rhythm close to that of ordinary speech), alternated with the choruses, which were always in lyric metres and usually arranged in *strophês* and *antistrophês* ('turns' and 'turnings back').

According to Aristotle, Sophocles introduced scene-painting (*skênographìa*) to suggest a visual background. Dead bodies could be displayed on a device called the *ekkuklêma*, a kind of stage truck which could be wheeled out from the central doors of the scene-building (*skênê*, literally 'tent'). In *Electra* this is how the dead body of Clytemnestra would have been displayed. A *mêchanê* ('machine', or mechanical crane) allowed aerial entrances and exits, usually of the gods, though it is seldom used by Sophocles in the plays of his which have survived.

Performance History

The more popular classical tragedies were often revived in the fourth century BC. During these revivals they were vulnerable to adaptation and additions by actors and producers. Around 330 BC, the Athenian politician Lycurgus prescribed that copies of the texts of the plays should be deposited in official archives, and that future performances should conform to these texts. These copies were lent to the Egyptian king, Ptolemy Euergetes I, and passed into the library at Alexandria, to form the basis of the critical edition made by the librarian, Aristophanes of Byzantium (ca. 257-180 BC). Although the performance tradition is not well documented for this period, the plays continued to be widely read, and scholars in Alexandria wrote commentaries on them, parts of which still survive. But by the second and third centuries AD, the number of plays that were being read had diminished. The seven plays of Aeschylus and the seven of Sophocles which survive were the only ones which were still available for performance. Of Euripides, there were ten such plays, but a further nine of his survive, preserved in a manuscript which presents them in a quasi-alphabetical order.

After the Athenian Academy was closed in 529 AD, classical texts and performance disappeared from sight for several centuries and did not re-emerge until the revival of learning in the early Byzantine period. Greek tragedy became known in the West mainly through Latin translations, and came to Shakespeare, for instance, via Seneca.

Sophocles' *Electra* was surprisingly neglected in revival until recent times. The production by Max Reinhardt in Berlin in 1903, 'translated' by Hugo von Hofmannsthal, is so free, it barely qualifies as a 'version' of Sophocles. There is no Tutor, no reported chariot-race, no urn even. The 'Electra complex' noted by Freud as an obsessive love for a father, seems to have made a contribution both to this new *Electra* and to the Richard Strauss opera for which von Hofmannsthal adapted his play into a libretto.

There was a production of the Sophocles in New York in 1909, directed by Isadora Duncan's brother, but that was in ancient Greek. In Greece, the play was directed by Dimitris Rondiris, originally with Katina Paxinou, then in 1962 with Aspasia Papathanassiou who was still working on the play as recently as 2002.

Michel St Denis directed the first revival of note in Britain just before the Second World War but productions, or adaptations, were thin on the ground anywhere until the 1980s.

Tadashi Suzuki took his *Clytemnestra* to Delphi, after it was performed in Toga, Japan in 1983. *Clytemnestra* combined Aeschylus' *Oresteia*, Sophocles' *Electra* and Euripides' *Electra* and *Orestes*. His *Electra* was performed at Delphi in 1995. He reduced and rearranged texts drastically. Suzuki stated that he wanted to show the breakdown of the family and family values in Japan.

Suzuki's Clytemnestra in the 1983 version was dressed in a traditional Japanese Noh costume, whereas the children wore informal Western clothing. Orestes threw the knife with which he killed his mother into a Marlboro wastebasket. Modern Japanese music was combined with music from Noh. The past mingled with the present, East with West.

In 1989, Andrei Serban's *An Ancient Trilogy*, including *Medea*, *Electra* and *Trojan Women*, was a symbolic protest against the Ceausescu oppression in Romania. He performed his piece in the original Greek so that the audience could not understand the language, but concentrated on the emotions and the visual action instead.

In the previous year, the production by Deborah Warner with Fiona Shaw in the title role had proved a much more faithful rendering of the original Sophoclean text. It was presented by the Royal Shakespeare Company in London in a translation by Kenneth McLeish, which Shaw herself later directed for radio. Warner's stage production concentrated on Electra as the centrepiece of the drama, with the plot almost taking second place. Sophocles' play encourages such an interpretation, and Shaw offered a distraught and self-destructive heroine, a wreck of a once noble princess reduced to an obsessive creature constantly washing in the trough of water that was a feature of the design.

Frank McGuinness's translation/version in 1997 of Sophocles' play toured England with Zoë Wanamaker as Electra in a production by David Leveaux, which also had great success in New York. Wanamaker had just lost her father, the celebrated actor and director Sam Wanamaker, a factor which seemed to fuel her impassioned performance.

A throbbing deep beat in the background greeted the audience. The set showed us something like Bosnia, devastated buildings, beside ancient ruins with a column overturned. The dress was modern Sarajevo with suggestions of Muslim women in the chorus with their hair covered. Electra appeared, with her hair in tatters: hunks cut out and bleeding sores on her scalp. She wore an overcoat that may have been Agamemnon's. Fog filled the stage, rain was falling and one drop splashed relentlessly down throughout the entire performance.

Mikis Theodorakis, who composed the music for Cacoyannis's film, *Electra*, (based more on the Euripides play, though with some elements from the Sophocles) also composed an opera on *Electra* in 1992. He varied the text freely, emphasising both themes of love and heroism: it owed as much to Sophocles as to Euripides, with a lot of Theodorakis.

Translators' Notes

Transliteration from ancient Greek into English is always imprecise, Greek having an alphabet of 24 letters, some of which have no single English equivalent. In Greek there is a 'k', but no 'c'; there are long and short 'o's (*ômega* and *omikron*) and 'e's (*êta* and *epsilon*); as well as single letters for 'th' (*thêta*), 'ph' (*phi*) and 'ch' (*chi*, pronounced as in the Scottish 'loch'). There is no letter 'h' but the 'h' sound can be represented by a 'breathing' mark above an initial letter. The present translators have followed their previous practice of opting for what is most likely to be familiar to the general reader, while acknowledging that the mixture of anglicisation and latinisation is not always consistent.

Lines in metrical portions, other than those in the iambic trimeters of dialogue, are capitalised throughout.

Ancient Greek has various expressions of grief or dismay, *Io moi moi, Pheu,* and so on. The translators have chosen to leave these as transliterations from the Greek rather than translate them into English as 'Woe is me' or 'Alas'. The reader should accept them as sounds indicating dismay. Directors may choose whatever way they feel appropriate to convey the feeling behind the sounds.

Marianne McDonald
University of California, San Diego

J. Michael Walton
University of Hull

For Further Reading

Blundell, N. W., *Helping Friends and Harming Enemies: A Study in Greek Ethics*, Cambridge, Cambridge University Press, 1989.

Foley, Helene, *Female Acts in Greek Tragedy*, Princeton, Princeton University Press, 2001.

Kirkwood, G. M., *A Study of Sophoclean Drama*, Ithaca, New York, Cornell University Press, 1958.

Kitto, H. D. F., *Sophocles: Dramatist and Philosopher*, Oxford, Oxford University Press, 1958.

Knox, B. M. W., *The Heroic Temper, Studies in Sophoclean Tragedy*, Berkeley, University of California Press, 1964.

Long, A. A., *Language and Thought in Sophocles*, London, Athlone Press, 1968.

McDonald, Marianne, *Ancient Sun, Modern Light: Greek Drama on the Modern Stage*, New York, Columbia University Press, 1992.

————— *Sing Sorrow: Classics, History, and Heroines in Opera*, Westport, Conn., Greenwood Press, 2001.

————— *The Living Art of Greek Tragedy*, Bloomington, Indiana, Indiana University Press, 2003.

Reinhardt, K., *Sophocles*, trans. Harvey Hazel and David Harvey, int. Hugh Lloyd-Jones, New York, Barnes & Noble, 1979.

Ringer, Mark, *Electra and the Empty Urn: Metatheatre and Role Play in Sophocles*, Chapel Hill, University of Carolina Press, 1998.

Stanford, W. B., *Tragedy and the Emotions: An Introductory Study*, New York, Routledge and Kegan Paul, 1983.

Walton, J. Michael, *Greek Theatre Practice*, Westport, Conn., Greenwood Press, 1980.

————— *Living Greek Theatre: A Handbook of Classical Performance and Modern Production*, Westport, Conn., Greenwood Press, 1987.

————— *The Greek Sense of Theatre: Tragedy Reviewed*, 2nd ed., London, Harwood Academic Publishers, 1996.

Webster, T. B. L., *An Introduction to Sophocles*. 1936; 2nd ed. London, Methuen, 1969.

Wiles, David, *Greek Theatre Performance: An Introduction*, Cambridge, Cambridge University Press, 2000.

Winnington-Ingram, R. P., *Sophocles: An Interpretation*, Cambridge, Cambridge University Press, 1980.

Woolf, Virginia, 'On Not Knowing Greek' in *The Common Reader*, 1925, rpt. New York, Harcourt, Brace, 1948.

Text and Edition

This translation has been prepared from the Oxford Text edited by H. Lloyd-Jones and N. G. Wilson, 1990; rpt. with corr. Oxford, Clarendon, 1992.

Jebb, J. B. ed. *Sophocles' Electra*, Cambridge, Cambridge University Press, 1894.

Kells, J. H., ed. Sophocles' *Electra*, Cambridge, Cambridge University Press, 1973.

Sophocles: Key Dates

NB All dates are BC; some are necessarily approximate; dates of some plays are unknown.

ca. 496	Sophocles born
490	First Persian War, Athenian victory at Marathon
480	Second Persian War; one of the dancers in the celebrations after Salamis
468	First dramatic competition, defeating Aeschylus
443/2	Treasurer *(Hellenotamias)* at Athens
441/0	General in Samian War
ca. 443-440	*Antigone*
ca. 442	*Ajax*
ca. 430s	*Women of Trachis*
431	Outbreak of the Peloponnesian War
430	Plague in Athens
ca. 420s	*King Oedipus*
ca.425-413	*Electra*, the same story as handled by both Aeschylus and Sophocles
415-13	Sicilian Expedition ending in Athenian defeat
413	One of the *Probouloi*, ten men, over 40 years old, appointed at Athens after the Sicilian defeat to run the city
409	*Philoctetes*
406	Death of Sophocles
404	End of Peloponnesian War
401	Posthumous performance of *Oedipus at Colonus*

ELECTRA

Characters

TUTOR

ORESTES, *son of Clytemnestra and Agamemnon*

PYLADES *(non-speaking), his friend*

ELECTRA, *sister of Orestes and Chrysothemis*

CHORUS *of Local Women*

CHRYSOTHEMIS

CLYTEMNESTRA

AEGISTHUS, *her new husband*

ATTENDANT *(non-speaking)*

Outside the palace at Mycenae. Enter TUTOR *with* ORESTES *and* PYLADES.

TUTOR

Orestes,
Son of Agamemnon who commanded the army at Troy,
now at last you can look on your heart's desire.
Here we are: Argos, your beloved city,
the holy place where Io, daughter of Inachus,
was driven by the gadfly of Hera.
And over here the agora of Apollo, killer of wolves;
there to the left, Hera's famous temple.
From where we're standing you can boast
you see Mycenae with all its gold,
and Pelops' palace with all its wealth of blood.
Your sister handed you over to me
and I took you far away from here.
I saved your life after your father's death,
and raised you up to be the strong man you are,
an avenger for your father.
Now, Orestes, and dear friend Pylades,
we must quickly make our plans.
Now the bright gleam of the sun
wakes the clear morning song of the birds,
and the dark night of stars has fled.
Now's the crucial moment, and the time to act;
we must seize it before the city stirs.

ORESTES

Dear old friend, you show me clearly
what a good and loyal man you are.

A thoroughbred, even if he's old,
is always there when you need him,
pricking up his ears and champing at the bit,
the first to encourage, and the first to follow us.
Here's what I'm planning to do.
Listen carefully and, if I'm off target, set me straight.
When I went to the oracle of Apollo,
to discover how best to take revenge for my father –
revenge on his killers that is my right and due –
here's what Apollo said:

*'Place not your trust in an army's sword or shield.
Use cunning. Kill them yourself and justly so.'*

Those were Apollo's very words.
So, when you get the chance, go inside the palace.
Find out what they are doing, and give us a full report.
No need to fear they'll recognise you,
you are too old and grey for that.
They won't be suspicious. Here's what you should say:
you're a Phocian stranger sent by Phanoteus,
their greatest ally.
Tell them on oath that Orestes is dead,
killed when he fell from his speeding chariot,
while competing in the Pythian Games.
That's your story.
And we shall visit my father's grave, as the god ordered,
to leave drink offerings and locks of hair.
Then we'll come back and pick up the bronze urn
which, you remember, we hid in the brush,
so that we can bring it back to support our story
and deliver the happy news that it contains my ashes.
There's no harm in saying that I am dead
when in fact I'm alive and about to win my fame.
No lie is bad if it achieves its purpose, I think.

I have known living wise men assumed dead,
who were honoured all the more on their return.
From this story, I'm sure it will be the same for me,
and I'll strike like lightning against my enemies.
O my country, gods of this place,
and you, my father's house,
give me good fortune as I go on my way,
for I come to right this wrong,
with Justice and the gods on my side.
Don't send me away from my country in shame,
but restore my fortune and my house.
Enough talk!
You, old man, do what you have to do,
and we'll be on our way.
Timing is everything: it makes or breaks
the affairs of men.

> ELECTRA *offstage.*

ELECTRA

Io moi moi!

TUTOR

That sounded like a servant crying indoors.

ORESTES

Could it be poor Electra? Should we wait and listen?

TUTOR

No. Let's not do anything before carrying out Apollo's
  orders.
Drink offerings on your father's grave: there's our starting
  point.
That should guarantee victory and success in all we do.

> *Exeunt* ORESTES, PYLADES, *and* TUTOR.
> *Enter* ELECTRA *from the palace, and, while she is speaking,*
> *the* CHORUS.

ELECTRA

O Light that is holy
And Air that equally blankets earth,
How many times you have heard my cries,
How many mournful songs,
And the sound of blows
That bloodied my breast
Whenever dark night slipped away.
My hateful bed is also witness
As I cry all night for my father. |
Ares, who loves bloodshed,
Did not invite him to rest in a barbarian land,
But my mother, and her bedmate Aegisthus,
Split open his head with a murderous axe
Just as a woodcutter splits an oak.
I am the only one to mourn poor Father,
Who died such a terrible death,
One deserving of pity.
I shall not stop weeping, or sobbing my agony, |
As long as I see stars shining in the heavens, |
Or the light of the dawning day,
Like the nightingale, Procne,
Who slew her own child,
Singing her sorrow endlessly
Before her father's doors
For all to hear.
Help me Hades and Persephone,
Hermes of Hell and Lady Curse,
Holy Furies, descended from gods,
And you who look on those who have died wrongly,
Who punish those who have violated marriage beds,
Come, help me avenge the murder of my father
And send my brother to me.
I can no longer bear it by myself.
The weight of grief crushes me down.

CHORUS

Child, child Electra,
Child of a terrible mother,
What endless sorrow consumes you?
You mourn for Agamemnon,
Destroyed in an ungodly trap
Your mother set,
Betrayed by her evil hand.
May the one that did this die,
If I may pray for such a thing.

ELECTRA

Good women
Who have come to comfort me,
I know all that you are trying to do,
And how you are offering help,
But I cannot stop crying for my poor father. |
I know you are the best of friends
And pay back kindness with kindness,
So I beg you to let me go my own way.

CHORUS

Your weeping is not going to bring back
Your father from the dead,
Nor will your prayers.
You are destroying yourself
With your immoderate and impossible grief,
Your endless moans.
Can't you see this will achieve nothing?
Why dedicate yourself to destruction?

ELECTRA

Only a fool would
Forget parents
Who deserve pity in their deaths.
I cannot forget the sorrow of Procne,

Who never gives up her cries of
'Itys' and again 'Itys',
Her ceaseless moans,
A nightingale mad from grief,
Messenger of Zeus.
And Niobe of the endless pain,
I count you a goddess,
You who shed tears forever
Down your tomb of rock.

CHORUS

You are not the only person to suffer, child.
There are those indoors
Who share your blood and ancestry,
Chrysothemis and Iphianassa.
Then there's Orestes,
Safe from sorrow,
Happy in his youth,
Distinguished by his birth,
Whom the famous land of the Myceneans
Will welcome when gracious Zeus
Brings him home at last.

ELECTRA

He's the one I wait for day after day,
I, who am childless, unwed, and drenched
In the tears of endless sorrow.
He's forgotten what he suffered and what I've told him.
Which of his messages has not been a lie?
For all the desire that he claims to have,
It is not enough to make him come here.

CHORUS

Don't give up, never give up, child.
Zeus is still in his heaven
And he oversees all and is ever-mighty;

Turn over to him your great anger weighted with pain;
Neither hate your enemies to excess,
Nor forget them.
Time heals everything.
The child of Agamemnon, who lives
In Crisa's pasture lands,
And the god who lords it over Acheron
Are not heedless of what happens.

ELECTRA

My life up to this point has been hopeless.
I'm losing my strength.
I'm withering away and I'm childless,
No close husband to stand by my side.
I live, a foreigner in my own house,
And serve in its rooms.
I wear filthy clothes
As I wait on tables
Which are empty for me.

CHORUS

The scream, horrible on his return,
Horrible in his home,
As the brazen axe
Delivered its straight blow.
Deceit was the teacher,
Love, the murderer:
The terrible created the terrible
In a deadly birth.
Was it god or man
That did it?

ELECTRA

That day was the worst day of all!
Night of the unspeakable feast,
Unbearable pain,

When my father died a horrible death
At both their hands:
That killed me likewise,
The hands of traitors.
May the great god of Olympus
Give them suffering in turn
In payment for their crime.
They should not enjoy the delights
But eat the evil fruit of their deeds.

CHORUS

No more.
Don't you understand where you are now
And how you got here?
You are making your own misery unbearable.
You set your soul at war with itself
And the evil demon of your anger is destroying you.
You cannot win against those in power.
Brace yourself, and wait.

ELECTRA

Terrible suffering brought me here
And forced me into terrible things.
I know my own anger.
As long as I must live with terror
I revel in my ruin.
No one with sense would
Advise me differently.
Words to console my spirit?
Hardly!
Spare me your good advice.
Leave!
This has no solution
And I will never stop weeping
Because my sorrows are numberless.

CHORUS

I wish you well,
Like a loving mother.
Don't let disaster
Breed disaster.

ELECTRA

And what limit is there to evil?
Is it right to have no concern for the dead?
That is not human.
I don't want honour from such callous people.
Spare me the good life in comfort.
I could never have peace if I stopped
The flight of my sharp-winged cries,
And dishonoured my father.
If he is to lie in earth,
Vanished into nothingness,
While they go free and unpunished,
Then there is no more shame
Or piety in the world of men.

CHORUS

I have come for your sake, child,
And for my own.
If what I say doesn't make sense,
Do what you like and we shall follow.

ELECTRA

Forgive me, kind friends.
I seem always to be complaining about something.
It does me no credit, but the life I lead gives me no option.
I'm sorry.
But how could any woman of royal blood
witness such catastrophe at home
and stand by doing nothing?
Evening and morning, that is what I've had to face,

each day more frightful than the last.
First my mother, the woman who gave me birth,
she hates me now.
I'm permitted to live out my life
in the house with my father's murderers.
They control me and make all my decisions for me.
Imagine, if you can, day in, day out,
watching Aegisthus squatting on my father's throne.
He wears my father's robes of state.
He pours drink offerings over the very hearth
where he cut my father down.
The final insult?
This killer lolls about in my father's bed,
alongside that foul mother of mine.
Mother, did I call her? Whore is a better word;
so sunk in depravity she lacks all fear of retribution.
She seems to luxuriate in what she's done,
ticking off each day on the calendar
till it's time to celebrate another month,
Another anniversary of scheming my father's murder,
which they celebrate with dancing and a sheep-feast
in honour of their household gods.
I have to watch all this, under my own roof.
That's why I weep! That's why I waste away,
mourning the vile celebration of my father's deathday.
I must keep silent, denied even the privilege of grief,
while she, in the most ladylike of tones,
calmly admonishes me, listing my faults;
'You really are a hateful child.
Are you the only girl who ever lost a father?
Have you a monopoly on grief?
To hell with you! Though the gods below
would be hard put to shut you up.'
That's the sort of thing she says,

except when she gets wind of Orestes.
Then it's 'This is all your fault',
and she rants and raves
'It was you – don't try to deny it –
stole him away from me.
But I warn you, you'll pay for it.'
That's what she barks at me,
while her esteemed husband eggs her on,
'the spineless one', that total disaster,
who can only wage war with a woman's help.
I have to bide my time, waiting for Orestes,
to come back and put a stop to all this.
I am dying of grief.
His constant delay has destroyed
my past and future hopes.
In a situation like this there's no room for logic,
good friends, nor for morality;
living with crime makes one a criminal.

CHORUS
Tell me, can Aegisthus hear you saying all this,
or is he away from the palace?

ELECTRA
Don't think I could be wandering around out here
if he were close by. He's away.

CHORUS
If that is the case, may I speak with you more frankly?

ELECTRA
What's on your mind?

CHORUS
I want to ask about your brother.
Will he come or not? I'd like to know.

ELECTRA

He says he will, but saying is not the same as doing.

CHORUS

A great task can take time.

ELECTRA

I didn't waste time when I saved his life.

CHORUS

Don't give up. He's a good man and he'll help his friends.

ELECTRA

You're right. Otherwise I'd be dead.

CHORUS

Don't say anything else.
I see Chrysothemis, coming from the house,
your sister born of the same father and mother.
She's carrying grave offerings,
the kind one gives to those below the earth.

Enter CHRYSOTHEMIS.

CHRYSOTHEMIS

Sister, what are you ranting about, out here in public again?
Haven't you learned your lesson by now?
Can't you see your anger gets you nowhere?
I know myself how I suffer and, had I the power,
I would let them know how I feel.
But in a storm, I prefer to lower my sails.
I'd rather not be blamed for something
that achieves nothing.
I wish you felt the same.
I know that your way is better than mine,
but I value my freedom, so I submit
in everything to those that have the power.

ELECTRA

It's a disgrace that you, a daughter of such a father,
    forget him,
and are just concerned for the woman who gave you birth.
Those are her words not yours.
All that lecture you've just given came from her, not you.
Make your choice: either be foolish, or be sensible
and betray those you love.
You said just now if you had the power
you'd tell them how you hated them,
but when I'm doing all I can to avenge my father,
you won't help, and even try to stop me.
Wouldn't this add cowardice to suffering?
Either you teach me, or you learn from me.
Why should I leave off mourning?
Am I not alive? A rotten life it may be, but it's enough
    for me.
I make trouble, and in this way I honour the dead,
assuming the dead enjoy such things.
Your hate is hate in words,
but the fact is you keep company with the murderers.
I'd never give in to them, even if they offered me
all those things that delight you so.
You can have the rich food and a life of luxury.
A clear conscience is food enough for me.
Your 'honour' is not one I'd like to share.
Neither would you, if you had any sense.
You could have been called the child of the finest father;
instead you are your mother's daughter.
For this, most people think you a traitor,
betraying your father and your family.

CHORUS

I beg you don't get angry!
There's some merit in what you both have to say.

You can learn from her, and she from you.

CHRYSOTHEMIS
I'm used to her talk. I wouldn't have said these things
if I hadn't heard news of a dreadful plan
which will stop her mourning for good.

ELECTRA
Tell me about this 'dreadful plan'.
If it's worse than what I suffer already,
I won't argue any more.

CHRYSOTHEMIS
I'll tell you what I know.
If you don't stop carrying on like this,
they will send you where you will never see sunlight again.
You'll be locked up far from your country,
where you can sing your dirges to your heart's content.
So give it some thought
and don't blame me later for what happens to you.
Now's the time for some straight thinking.

ELECTRA
Is that what they are planning for me?

CHRYSOTHEMIS
Yes they are! As soon as Aegisthus gets home.

ELECTRA
The sooner the better as far as I'm concerned.

CHRYSOTHEMIS
What are you saying?

ELECTRA
I want him back if that is what he has in mind.

CHRYSOTHEMIS
Why? Are you out of your mind?

ELECTRA

So that I can get as far away from all of you as possible.

CHRYSOTHEMIS

What about the life you would be leaving here?

ELECTRA

What life? Is my life here so wonderful?

CHRYSOTHEMIS

It could be if only you'd be sensible.

ELECTRA

Don't tell me to betray those I love.

CHRYSOTHEMIS

That's not what I'm telling you; I'm telling you to submit
to authority.

ELECTRA

You do that; that's not my way.

CHRYSOTHEMIS

It's right not to destroy yourself through stupidity.

ELECTRA

I'll destroy myself if I must, to avenge my father.

CHRYSOTHEMIS

But Father understands what we're up against and would
forgive us.

ELECTRA

That's a coward talking.

CHRYSOTHEMIS

Is there no way I can convince you?

ELECTRA

No. I hope I would never be that stupid.

CHRYSOTHEMIS

Then I'll go and do what I was asked.

ELECTRA

Where are you going with those offerings?

CHRYSOTHEMIS

Mother has sent them for Father's grave.

ELECTRA

What? For her worst enemy?

CHRYSOTHEMIS

The man she killed. That's what you'd rather say?

ELECTRA

On whose suggestion? Why now?

CHRYSOTHEMIS

She had a nightmare, I think.

ELECTRA

Gods of my ancestors, help me now!

CHRYSOTHEMIS

So her fear encourages you?

ELECTRA

Tell me the dream and I'll let you know.

CHRYSOTHEMIS

I can tell what I know, but it's not much.

ELECTRA

Tell me anyway.
The smallest word can make or break a man.

CHRYSOTHEMIS

The word is that she saw Father,
That he was back with her, alive again;

he took the staff that he used to carry,
which Aegisthus holds now, and planted it in the hearth.
It grew many branches and leaves until it covered all
    Mycenae.
This at least is what someone told me
who overheard her telling the Sun her dream.
That's all I know except that that's why she's sending me:
She's scared.
I beg you not to do anything foolish;
Don't push me away now. Later will be too late.

ELECTRA

Dear Sister, don't put any of what you are carrying
on the tomb. Neither gods nor men think it right
that you give sacred offerings to our father
from a woman who hated him;
throw them to the winds or bury them,
deep in the dust and far from his resting place.
They'll be her keepsakes down below for when she dies.
Anyway, she is quite shameless to send such tasteless
    offerings
to adorn the grave of a man she murdered.
How grateful do you think that corpse in the tomb will be
for gifts from a woman who killed and dishonoured him?
She cut off his extremities as if he were an enemy
and wiped her hands on his head to clean off the blood.
Surely, you don't think that this will free her from guilt?
That's impossible. Throw them away.
Cut the ends of your own hair, and of mine –
poor gifts though they are, they're the best I can do –
and give them to him:
hair without shine and a belt without ornament.
Fall on your knees and pray that he rise
from beneath the earth to help us,
and that his son Orestes be alive and come

to overwhelm and trample on our enemies,
so that we may one day honour him
with richer hands than those that serve him now.
I think, yes, I think *he* sent his haunting dream to her.
In any case, do make these offerings for both our sakes,
and for our beloved father lying in Hades.

CHORUS
Her words honour the gods, and if you have any sense,
you will do just what she says.

CHRYSOTHEMIS
I'll do it. If something is right,
joint action is better than two opposed opinions.
Please friends, keep quiet about what I'm trying to do.
If my mother hears anything,
I'm afraid I'll regret my recklessness.

Exit CHRYSOTHEMIS.

CHORUS
If I'm not a mad prophet,
Lacking any sense,
Justice tells me
That a fair victory will carry the day,
And we don't have long to wait, child.
Confidence fills me
As I inhale
The sweet scent of that dream
I heard about.
The lord of the Greeks,
Your father,
Will never forget,
Nor will the ancient bronze axe
Of the double blade
Which slew him
In most outrageous shame.

With her many feet and many claws
She scuttles out of her hiding place,
Deadly Erinys of the brazen talons.
She attacks those criminals
Who lusted after a blood-stained marriage,
A wedding, without wedding,
A bed, without rest or love.
That's why I'm sure
That a divine sign will never,
No never, come to bless
Those who did the deed
And their accomplices.
I'll never again believe in prophecy
Or fearsome dreams, or oracles,
If this vision of the night
Fails to turn out well.

That chariot race of Pelops, long ago,
Horsemanship of sorrow,
Day in and day out,
You bring pain to this land.
Since Myrtilus drowned,
Lulled to sleep by the sea,
When he fell from his golden chariot,
Hurled headlong in shameful misery,
Never has this house
Been free from shame and suffering.

Enter CLYTEMNESTRA *with* ATTENDANT *carrying
offerings.*

CLYTEMNESTRA

So, you're out here again, are you,
just because Aegisthus is away?
At least he kept you safe indoors,
not out here, shaming your loved ones.

With him not here, you can slander me more freely.
You've told everyone so often what a tyrant I am,
my brazen rule flouting all justice
always abusing you and yours.
I've never abused you, unless repaying
insult with insult can be termed abuse.
As for that father of yours, your excuse for all this,
yes, I admit it – he was killed by me,
by me, and well I know it!
You won't find me trying to deny it.
But not just by me, by me and by Justice.
It's best having Justice on your side, you'll find.
This father you are always weeping for
was the only Greek to make your sister, Iphigenia,
a human sacrifice to the gods. No grief for him!
He begot her. I was the one gave birth.
Well then, tell me, please, why did he do it?
Why did he sacrifice her? 'For the Greeks', did you say?
What right had they to kill a child – my child?
For his brother Menelaus, then – of course.
And should he not pay recompense to me for that?
Menelaus had two children? What about them?
Shouldn't they have been the ones to die,
their father and mother, Helen and Menelaus, being who
    they were?
The whole expedition was about Helen!
Did Death want to gorge on my child above hers?
Had he no love for my children, only those of Menelaus?
The man was a monster! Wouldn't you say he was wrong-
    headed?
Foolish, at the very least? I think so, even if you don't agree.
The one who is dead would agree, if she could speak.
I don't regret what was done. And if you think me wrong,
learn about Justice before you blame another.

ELECTRA

You can't blame me this time for starting the quarrel.
It was you. But, if you allow,
I would like to set some things straight,
about the dead man and my sister too.

CLYTEMNESTRA

I give you permission. If you had always begun so
    reasonably,
it would have been easier for me to listen to you.

ELECTRA

Very well then. You admit you killed my father.
Could anything be worse than that, whether it was just
    or not?
Not that you did kill him justly;
you were persuaded by that evil lover of yours.
Ask Artemis why she held back the winds at Aulis.
I'll tell you since we can't ask her directly.
As the story goes, my father was hunting in her sacred grove
when his footstep flushed out a horned and dappled stag.
As he killed it he made some boastful remark.
This angered Artemis and she held back the winds
until Father sacrificed his own daughter in recompense for
    the animal.
That was the reason for the sacrifice, otherwise the army
could neither have returned home nor gone on to Troy.
He was forced into this sacrifice. It was the last thing
    he wanted.
He did *not* do it for Menelaus. And even if he had,
taking your point, was that a reason to kill him?
What law says that? Take care if you're going to invent
    a law
which might backfire on you and cause you pain.
Take a life for a life, you'd be the first to die under such
    a law.

I think you are just looking for an excuse.
So please tell me why you are committing the worst crime
    now.
You're sharing a bed with your accomplice in the murder.
You're having his children, but you threw out the proper
    children
of the proper father. How could I condone this?
Would you claim it's compensation for a daughter lost?
Shocking, if that's what you are saying;
horrible to sleep with the enemy for your daughter's sake.
But I'm not allowed to criticise you
because you always say I'm condemning my mother.
Let's face it, you are more of a master than a mother,
and I lead a horrible life, constantly abused by you and
    your lover;
and the other one barely escaped,
poor Orestes, who wastes away his unhappy life.
You accuse me so often of raising him to take vengeance,
and, believe me, I would have if I could.
Call me anything you like: bad, foul-mouthed or shameless.
I'm an expert in all of that: I'm my mother's daughter.

CHORUS

I see how furious she makes you, but
Whether she is justified is something you don't consider.

CLYTEMNESTRA

Why should I consider that when all she does
is insult her mother? And at her age!
She's so shameless; she's capable of anything.

ELECTRA

I feel shame – you should realise that –
even if you don't think so.
I also know why my behaviour seems inappropriate
and I'm forced to act against my own nature.

Your animosity and actions in the past compel me:
wickedness breeds wickedness.

CLYTEMNESTRA
You insolent bitch! What I've said and done
has given you too much freedom.

ELECTRA
Your words, not mine. You have done what you did,
and actions speak louder than words.

CLYTEMNESTRA
By Artemis, you'll pay for this impertinence.
Just wait until Aegisthus gets home.

ELECTRA
See? You gave me permission to speak freely,
but you lose your temper: you don't know how to listen.

CLYTEMNESTRA
Won't you allow me to conduct this sacrifice in peace,
now that I have let you have your say?

ELECTRA
I allow you; please do sacrifice! Don't worry,
I'll keep quiet. I won't say another word.

CLYTEMNESTRA (to ATTENDANT)
You there, raise up these offerings of fruit,
so that my prayers to this god may free me from my fears.
Apollo, my protector, hear my silent prayer.
I'm not speaking among friends,
so it's not right to reveal everything in her presence.
Her hatred for me may encourage her
to spread idle gossip throughout the city.
Listen to me. This is what I have to say.
If the visions that I saw in my uncertain dreams
were favourable, Lord of Lycia, then bring them to pass.

If they were not, turn them back against my enemies.
If anyone is plotting to take away the wealth I have,
prevent it, but let me live my life without harm,
ruling over the house of Atreus and all around it,
with the friends who now surround me,
living each day in happiness with those of my children
who bear no grudge against me and cause me no pain.
Hear this graciously, Apollo, and grant us what we ask.
All the rest, even if I say nothing,
you know because you are a god.
I'm sure the children of Zeus see all things.

Enter TUTOR.

TUTOR
Ladies of this land, would you be so good as to tell me
whether this is the palace of King Aegisthus?

CHORUS
Yes, sir, it is. As you have guessed.

TUTOR
And would I be right in assuming that that is his wife?
She certainly has a regal air.

CHORUS
None more so. That is the queen.

TUTOR
My greetings, Madam. I have news for you from a friend,
good news for you and for your husband, Aegisthus.

CLYTEMNESTRA
I thank you for your greeting. But first of all
I would like to know who it was that sent you here.

TUTOR
Phanoteus the Phocian, with an important message.

CLYTEMNESTRA

What sort of message? Tell me. I know him,
and since the man's a friend, his message must be friendly.

TUTOR

Orestes is dead: that's it in short.

ELECTRA

No! Then today I die too.

CLYTEMNESTRA

What did you say, stranger? What did you say? Pay no
attention to her.

TUTOR

I said it then and I'll say it again. Orestes is dead.

ELECTRA

I'm destroyed, totally destroyed. Electra is no more.

CLYTEMNESTRA

You keep out of this.
Stranger, tell me the truth. How did he die?

TUTOR

That's why I was sent here, and I'll tell you everything.
Orestes had gone to Delphi to compete for prizes
in the famous Pythian Games.
When he heard the loud cry announcing the first race,
our distinguished Orestes entered the course
and was seen in his glory by everyone present.
He was as successful as he was handsome
and walked off with the coveted trophy.
To make a long story short, I don't know anyone
who could match him in skill or in achievement;
in every set event, he carried off the prize
and everyone cheered each time the announcement came:
'The Argive wins, Orestes, son of Agamemnon,

leader of the famous Greek army.' So that's how things
   were.
But if a god is up to no good, not even a strong man can
   escape.

Next day, at sunrise, was a swift-footed chariot race,
Which Orestes entered with other charioteers.
One was an Achaean; one from Sparta;
two from Libya driving yoked chariots.
Then came Orestes, fifth, with a team of Thessalian horses.
Sixth, was an Aetolian with sorrel colts;
a man from Magnesia seventh; the eighth, an Aenian,
had white horses; the ninth's from Athens, the city built
   by gods;
another from Boeotia drove the tenth chariot.
They lined up in the position the judges had assigned
   by lot.
A blast from the bronze trumpet was the signal to start,
and they were off like the wind.
The drivers shouted to their horses and shook their reins.
The whole course was filled with the rattle of hurtling
   chariots.
Dust rose to the sky and the chariots were crammed
   together;
no one spared the whip, each striving to get a wheel ahead
and pass the snorting horses alongside them.
Their backs and wheels were sprayed
with the foam of panting horses.

At each turning point, Orestes hugged the pillar,
scraping close to it, giving free rein to the outer trace-horse,
checking the inner one to block off the pursuer.
At first all the drivers stood securely in their chariots.
Then the ill-disciplined horses of the Aenian bolted
and, at the beginning of the seventh lap,

crashed head-on into one of the Libyans.
Then one smashed against another creating total disaster.
Soon all the plain of Crisa was filled with wreckage.
The clever Athenian, seeing this, drove aside and slowed
    down.
This way he avoided crashing into the chariots
piled-up in the middle of the course.

Orestes was last at the time, holding back his team,
confident in the outcome. When he saw there was only
    one left,
he gave a sharp command into the ears of his swift horses,
and set off in pursuit. They were neck and neck,
now one ahead, now the other.
Through every lap so far, our poor Orestes
had kept his course steady and his chariot safe.
But this time as the horses rounded the turn
he slackened the left rein and before he knew it,
struck the edge of the pillar. The axle box shattered.
He went head first over the handrail, and got tangled
    in the reins.
As he hit the ground, the horses panicked and ran across
    the course.

The spectators saw him fall from his chariot
and cried out in pity for this young man
who'd had such success, but now such suffering,
first dragged across the ground, then bouncing, his feet
    in the air.
Charioteers managed to stop the runaway horses with
    difficulty.
They released his mangled body, covered with blood,
unrecognisable to even his closest friends.

They built a pyre and burnt him on it.
His huge body was reduced to miserable ashes

and placed in a small bronze urn.
Phocians were appointed to bring it here,
so he could be buried in the land of his fathers.
That is what happened, painful to put into words,
but worse for us that witnessed it.
In fact, it is the worst disaster I have ever seen.

CHORUS

Pheu! Pheu!
Our master's ancient line is utterly destroyed.

CLYTEMNESTRA

Zeus, how do I describe what's happened?
Fortunate? Disastrous? Convenient perhaps?
How sad, if it takes adversity to save my life.

TUTOR

Why does this news upset you so, lady?

CLYTEMNESTRA

Being a mother is a strange thing;
no matter how badly they treat you,
you can't hate your children.

TUTOR

It seems my coming here was a mistake.

CLYTEMNESTRA

Not at all. How can you call it a mistake
if you came bringing me proof of my son's death?
He was my child, whom I nursed at my breast,
before he left me for another land.
After he left home he never saw me again.
He blamed me for his father's murder,
and made terrible threats about what he would do.
Sweet sleep escaped me day and night,
and I lived as if every moment were to be my last.

But now, from this day on,
I'm no longer afraid of him – or her.
She was worse because she lived with me
and sucked the life-blood out of me.
Now we can live in peace, free from her threats.

ELECTRA

I'm finished! Now I have to mourn you, Orestes,
while my mother shows contempt for your death.
How right can that be?

CLYTEMNESTRA

Not right for you, perhaps, but right for him.

ELECTRA

Nemesis, do you hear how she speaks of the dead?

CLYTEMNESTRA

Nemesis heard what she had to hear and made the right
  decision.

ELECTRA

Heap insults on me; now you have the chance.

CLYTEMNESTRA

Aren't you and Orestes going to stop me?

ELECTRA

We can't stop you. We're the ones who've been stopped.

CLYTEMNESTRA (to TUTOR)

You would certainly deserve a reward, dear friend,
if you put a stop to that strident tongue of hers.

TUTOR

I've done all I can. I'll leave now.

CLYTEMNESTRA

I won't hear of it. That would not be proper for me,

nor show proper respect to the friend who sent you.
Do come in. We'll leave her out here with her friends
to scream out all her sufferings to her heart's content.

Exeunt into the palace CLYTEMNESTRA *and* TUTOR.

ELECTRA

Does that look to you like a grief-stricken mother,
who is mourning her dead son, weeping bitter tears,
wailing, and in agony? No, she's gone off, laughing to
   herself.
God, I hate her. Dear Orestes, your death has killed me.
You've torn from my heart the last fond hope I had
of vengeance for my father and for me.
Now where do I turn from here?
I'm all alone. I have no brother. I have no father.
I have to serve those whom I most hate,
My father's murderers. Can this be right?
But I shall not live with them for the rest of my years.
Instead I'd rather walk away, through that gate,
and grind out my life alone.
If that bothers anyone indoors, he can kill me.
Death would be welcome when living means only sorrow.
I've lost the will to live.

CHORUS

Where is Zeus' lightning,
Helios, and the sun's bright eye to see all this?
Can they look on impassively,
colluding to conceal it?

ELECTRA

E e, ai ai!

CHORUS

Child, why do you cry out?

ELECTRA
Pheu!

CHORUS
Your grief should be more moderate.

ELECTRA
You're adding to my pain.

CHORUS
How?

ELECTRA
If you try to suggest hope for me
In those who have gone to Hades,
You will bury me a second time.

CHORUS
I know how King Amphiaraus,
Was buried in the earth
Killed by the glitter of
A woman's golden necklace . . .

ELECTRA
E e, io!

CHORUS
A king, with all the powers of a seer.

ELECTRA
Pheu!

CHORUS
Pheu, she who killed him . . .

ELECTRA
Was killed in turn.

CHORUS
Yes.

ELECTRA

I know. I know. An avenger appeared
To champion the mourner.
But none for me.
He is dead and gone.

CHORUS

You are a woman of sorrows
One follows after the other.

ELECTRA

I know this. I know it all too well.
Suffering weaves a pattern in my life,
Sorrow after sorrow
Day after day and month after month.

CHORUS

We have seen all these sorrows.

ELECTRA

Don't lead me down a path where there is no . . .

CHORUS

No what?

ELECTRA

No hope of help from noble relatives.

CHORUS

Death comes to everyone.

ELECTRA

Not like his, my poor brother,
Caught and dragged by the reins
In that contest of flashing hooves.

CHORUS

Unspeakable violence.

ELECTRA

Yes. A stranger in a strange land
Without even the touch of my hand...

CHORUS

Aiai!

ELECTRA

He has died and has no tomb,
No funeral prayers from us....

Enter CHRYSOTHEMIS.

CHRYSOTHEMIS

Dearest Sister, I've run all the way here:
undignified, perhaps, but spurred on by happiness.
I have wonderful news for you,
an end to everything that's happened,
all you've suffered.

ELECTRA

Where could you have found a cure for incurable
suffering?

CHRYSOTHEMIS

Orestes has come – are you listening to me?
As truly as you see me standing here.

ELECTRA

Are you out of your mind, you poor fool,
to make fun of your own troubles, never mind mine?

CHRYSOTHEMIS

No, I'm serious. I swear by our father's house!
He's here, I tell you.

ELECTRA

I can't bear it. Who was it told you this,
this story you are far too willing to believe?

CHRYSOTHEMIS

I trusted only myself, no one else —
clear proof and the evidence of my own eyes.

ELECTRA

Proof, you poor fool? What proof?
What vision has provoked your fevered imagination?

CHRYSOTHEMIS

Just listen, for heaven's sake! Then make up your mind
whether it's my 'fevered imagination'.

ELECTRA

Alright. Tell me, if it will make you happy.

CHRYSOTHEMIS

I mean to — everything I've seen.
When I reached our father's tomb,
I saw that fresh milk had been poured over the mound,
and flowers of all kinds garlanded around the headstone.
It was an amazing sight and I looked around carefully
in case someone was nearby watching me.
But nothing stirred, so I stole closer to the tomb.
There on the edge of the grave was a lock of hair,
newly cut. The moment I saw it
I had this premonition in my heart.
This was a sign. It had to be Orestes,
whom I love more than anyone alive.
I picked up the hair without a word,
and suddenly my eyes filled with tears of joy.
It was his. I knew it then. I know it now.
This treasure could have come from none but him.
Apart from you or me, who could have put it there?
It wasn't me, I know. It wasn't you either.
How could it have been when you're not allowed
to leave the house even to sacrifice to the gods?

Mother? It's not her way to do that sort of thing.
Anyway, we'd have seen her.
This offering can only have been from Orestes.
So, dear one, take heart. The path of destiny can change,
this way or that. Till now she has scowled on us.
Today is a new day and better times are here perhaps.

ELECTRA

Pheu! How little you know. I pity you.

CHRYSOTHEMIS

What's the matter? Isn't this good news?

ELECTRA

You can't tell fact from fantasy.

CHRYSOTHEMIS

You want me to doubt what I have seen?

ELECTRA

He is dead. He won't save you.
Don't expect anything from him.

CHRYSOTHEMIS

That's terrible. Who told you this?

ELECTRA

Someone who was there when he died.

CHRYSOTHEMIS

Where is this man? I can't believe it.

ELECTRA

He's in the house, my mother's welcome guest for his
    good news.

CHRYSOTHEMIS

Terrible. But then what about all those burial offerings
at the grave? Who brought them?

ELECTRA

I suppose someone left them there
in memory of the dead Orestes.

CHRYSOTHEMIS

This is a disaster.
Here I was rushing to bring you good news,
unaware of our calamity. But now that I'm here,
I find we're worse off than before.

ELECTRA

So that's how it is. But if you do what I say,
you will make our suffering easier to bear.

CHRYSOTHEMIS

Do you want me to raise him from the dead?

ELECTRA

That's not what I was saying! I'm not an idiot.

CHRYSOTHEMIS

Tell me something that I can do.

ELECTRA

Have the courage to do what I ask.

CHRYSOTHEMIS

If I can help, I will.

ELECTRA

No success without hard work.

CHRYSOTHEMIS

I know that. I'll do as much as I can.

ELECTRA

Listen and I'll tell you what I'm planning.
You know as well as I do we've no friend left to help us.
Death has taken them and we're left alone.

As long as I thought our brother was still alive and well,
I had hope that he would come and avenge our father's
     murder.
But now that he's gone, I'm turning to you.
Don't be afraid to join your sister in killing Aegisthus,
the murderer of our father.
There. I've said it all. No secrets any more.
Why do you hesitate? You can't simply do nothing.
What hope is left for us?
Do you want to sit around for the rest of your life
complaining about your lost inheritance
and that you're not married and not likely to be?
Don't expect marriage. Aegisthus is not so brainless as
     to let us
bear children who would clearly make trouble for him.
If you listen to me and do what I say,
to begin with, you will get credit for devotion
both from our dead father and our brother.
Secondly, you'll be called free for all time
and that's your birthright.
Then you will be able to make a fine marriage.
Everyone admires courage.
Don't you realise how if you go along with me,
you will enhance the reputation of us both?
What local or what foreigner on seeing us,
will not be full of praise, saying,
'Look at those two sisters, friends,
how they fearlessly avenged murder,
and restored their father's house,
despite their powerful enemies.
They deserve love. They deserve respect from all.
Everyone should honour them for their courage
both at public feasts and civic assemblies.'
That's how men will speak of us, and our fame

will be immortal among the living and the dead.
So, my dear, do what I say and work together with your
    father.
Strive, along with your brother.
Put an end to my suffering, yours as well, and know this:
a shameful life shames nobility.

CHORUS
In matters like this, forethought is an ally
for those who speak and those who listen.

CHRYSOTHEMIS
If she had any sense, she would have exercised some
    discretion
before she gave that speech, but she didn't.
What possessed you to pursue such a rash course
and expect me to help?
Can't you see? You are just a woman, not a man,
and not as strong as your enemies.
Their strength increases day by day,
while ours ebbs away to nothing.
Who could plot to kill a man like him
and hope to get away with it scot-free?
Don't you realise, if someone heard what we said,
our bad situation could become a disaster?
We win nothing if we gain a fine reputation
and stupidly lose our lives in the process.
Dying isn't the worst thing, but when one
wants to die, being unable to.
So, I beg you, restrain your temper
before you ruin everything and destroy our family.
I'll pretend I never heard what you said,
And, while there's still time, you should learn:
when you have no power yourself, obey those who have.

CHORUS

She's right. There is nothing better than
thinking ahead and thinking clearly.

ELECTRA

What you said was no surprise.
I knew you would reject my plan . . .
I have to do this alone now.
I'll not give up.

CHRYSOTHEMIS

Pheu!
If only you had shown such determination
When Father died,
You'd have won the day.

ELECTRA

I was the same Electra then, but I'm wiser now.

CHRYSOTHEMIS

Pray god you stay as wise as you were then.

ELECTRA

So you'll lecture me, but you won't help me.

CHRYSOTHEMIS

You'll never get away with it!

ELECTRA

I envy your good sense, but hate your cowardice.

CHRYSOTHEMIS

I'll listen, and one day, perhaps, you will admit that I was
right.

ELECTRA

Never. That's one thing you will never hear from me.

CHRYSOTHEMIS

Wait, just wait. There's lots of time and only time will tell.

ELECTRA

Go away. You're no help.

CHRYSOTHEMIS

I am. But you won't listen.

ELECTRA

Go and tell Mother everything.

CHRYSOTHEMIS

Of course not! I'm not your enemy and I don't hate you.

ELECTRA

I see how you despise me.

CHRYSOTHEMIS

I don't despise you. I'm trying to protect you.

ELECTRA

Am I to accept your definition of what is right?

CHRYSOTHEMIS

Yes, if you're sensible. And then I'll go along with you.

ELECTRA

It is a terrible thing to speak well, but be wrong.

CHRYSOTHEMIS

That's exactly your problem.

ELECTRA

What do you mean? Do you deny what I say is right?

CHRYSOTHEMIS

Sometimes being right can be dangerous.

ELECTRA

I don't want to live by your sort of rules.